EXPLORATIONS

poems by

Gregory A. Ashe

Finishing Line Press
Georgetown, Kentucky

EXPLORATIONS

For my wife, Jordana

You are the beauty my eye beholds.
You are all I desire.
You are the one who can calm my soul.
You set my heart on fire.

Copyright © 2018 by Gregory A. Ashe
ISBN 978-1-63534-727-2 First Edition
All rights reserved under International and Pan-American Copyright Conventions. No part of this book may be reproduced in any manner whatsoever without written permission from the publisher, except in the case of brief quotations embodied in critical articles and reviews.

ACKNOWLEDGMENTS

I would like to thank the editors of *Fredericksburg Literary and Art Review* where *Appalachian Dawn* originally appeared.

I would like to thank LB Sedlacek for her incredibly helpful comments. I would also like to thank the late Dr. Eliot Blum (of blessed memory) who encouraged me to turn my thoughts into poetry.

The reader may recognize the last line of *Rotunda Dreams*, which comes from Hamlet's soliloquy in Act III, Scene 1 of Shakespeare's *Hamlet*. *Western Explorations* opens and closes with passages from Walt Whitman's *Song of the Open Road*. *Delicate Arch*, which is part of *Western Explorations*, concludes with a quote from the final verse of John Milton's *Paradise Lost*. In *Double Arch*, I include an exchange between a young man and an old man that is based on a scene from the 1970s television series *Kung Fu*. Meanwhile, throughout *Western Explorations*, I make reference to several proverbs and sayings that I recall reading on National Park Service or other signage.

Publisher: Leah Maines
Editor: Christen Kincaid
Cover Art: Gregory A. Ashe
Author Photo: Gregory A. Ashe
Cover Design: Elizabeth Maines McCleavy

Printed in the USA on acid-free paper.
Order online: www.finishinglinepress.com
        also available on amazon.com

        Author inquiries and mail orders:
        Finishing Line Press
        P. O. Box 1626
        Georgetown, Kentucky 40324
        U. S. A.

Table of Contents

Rotunda Dreams 1

Western Explorations 4

Appalachian Dawn 29

Writing was unknown to early man, and poetry was far better
adapted to be retained in the mind...
The first writing to be preserved by man is poetry.

My Great Aunt Birdie Lazarus
A Garden of Thoughts

It's these little things, they can pull you under.
Live your life filled with joy and wonder.
I always knew this altogether thunder,
Was lost in our little lives.
Oh, but sweetness follows.

R.E.M.
Sweetness Follows

INTRODUCTION

Welcome, gentle reader, and thank you for taking time to read my poetry chapbook. I hope you enjoy it. I thought a few words of introduction about my poems might be useful.

Rotunda Dreams originated from musings while I sat on the steps of Thomas Jefferson's Rotunda at the University of Virginia in Charlottesville. I had but a few weeks left before I graduated from the Law School. It was a beautifully warm spring evening, and I sat and wrote what came to mind.

Western Explorations arose from my notes during a 30-day solo tour of several National Parks in the American West. Many law students travel during the month between taking the bar exam at the end of July and starting their jobs at the end of August. Many of my friends were touring Europe or Asia or some other exotic locale. My sights, and wallet, were more modest. I booked flights from Washington, D.C. to Salt Lake City to Seattle and back to D.C. and rented a small car with unlimited mileage. Other than a week backpacking excursion in Glacier National Park and a three-day rafting trip down the Green River in Dinosaur National Monument, I had nowhere I had to be.

Appalachian Dawn was inspired by a trip I made over a Labor Day weekend. I had only just started working at a law firm and was living in Washington, D.C. A dear friend was getting married on a mountaintop in West Virginia. I had my journal with me, and stopped every now and then along the drive as the mood struck.

Rotunda Dreams

It is pleasantly warm,
sitting on the steps of the Rotunda
gazing out at the darkened Lawn.
All is quiet save for isolated conversations of couples
and small groups of students nearby.
I hear the distant sounds of a radio from one of the Lawn rooms.

The lights of the Rotunda are a distraction,
obscuring my view of the million stars above.
But the soft, hazy glow of the lights
is beautiful.

A couple sits to my left,
laying back on the steps
staring up at the stars.
Behind me, on the portico,
students try to identify the constellations.
Perhaps I could introduce myself.
"Hello," I could say.
"You know I graduated from here with a degree in Astronomy."
I could point out all the stars . . .
Instead, I remain quiet,
and just listen.

A woman to my left laughs.
I wonder what her companion said that is so amusing.
It is a nice laugh,
a pleasant soothing sound.
Alas, they get up and leave.
Au revoir.

Scattered about the Lawn,
I see one, two, maybe three couples lying on the grass.
It is hard to tell
as the darkness quickly engulfs all but the nearby.

The air is pleasantly warm.
A slight breeze comes every now and then
bringing the slightest chill.

The students continue to discuss astronomy.
Strangely, even today we remain captivated by the stars.
How much more so our primitive ancestors,
gazing at the strange points of light hanging in the sky.
Some cultures thought of stars as campfires,
the whole sky nothing but tribes
sitting around campfires.
There is a comforting universalness to that thought.
Instead of vainly placing themselves at the center of a universe
built exclusively for them,
They saw themselves as one piece in a vast cosmic scheme.
To any other campfire, they knew that they too
were just another point of light.

Two women step onto the Lawn,
one stopping to take her sandals off
feeling the cool grass underfoot.
Both wear dresses of bright yellow and green,
still the darkness covers them,
taking them from my sight
as they walk down the Lawn.
Six people approach up the Lawn.
I see them in silhouette,
backlit from the lights of distant Cabell Hall.
Like Dorothy's arrival in Oz,
they appear in full color
and enter the soft glow of the Rotunda.

A couple to my left lies on the grass.
One lights up a cigarette.
For an instant, the flame looks like a small star shining in the dark.
Just for an instant.
No wonder our ancestors thought stars were campfires.

Someday I will read these words
and remember the simple life of a student.
I can read and remember that life is still simple
and slow
and warm
and hazy
and dim
in the soft glow of the Rotunda's lights.

The clock nears midnight.
Fraternity boys run past
streaking the Lawn.
Two women stand watching
in the purple shadows of the Rotunda.
I hear them debate whether to join in.
One undresses down to her undergarments,
before they decide against making the attempt.
Oh well.
I watch them wander away
fully clothed.

It is past midnight.
I am alone.
I sit and gaze out into the empty darkness
and smile.
I take a few more breaths of the warm night air,
then amble off to find my bed
and there to sleep.
To sleep: perchance to dream . . .

Western Explorations

Afoot and light-hearted I take to the open road,
Healthy, free, the world before me,
The long brown path before me leading wherever I choose...

Great Salt Lake

Antelope Island
largest in the Great Salt Lake.
I overlook a small cove.
The beach salt-white from evaporation.
The smell is incredible
—pure salt!
In the distance, I see veils of water vapor
evaporating off the lake surface.
Amazing!
Reverse rain!

Alpine Junction

The great Snake River plain stretches before me.
The Caribou Range to my right,
in the distance, the Sawtooths of middle Idaho.

I enter Swan Valley and cross a boundary
between Southwest and Northwest.
Before, all is brown.
Mountains rocky with few trees
(except for snow still on some peaks).
Now, all is green.
Mountains filled with pine.
Desert turns to forest.
I smell the fir trees.
I close my eyes
and remember the tree-in-a-bucket I bought at Big Meadows as a child.

I pass a lake.
The water is bluer than blue
reflecting bluer than blue sky.
The Snake River digs small green canyons alongside the road,
other times it is valley.
But all is verdant and cool, dark green.
And the fir trees forever march up the slopes of the mountains.

Grand Tetons

I look east over Jenny Lake
and the Snake River valley and the next range of mountains beyond.
To my right, left, and behind,
Teton peaks stab skyward into the blue of the sky.
The glaciers still on the peaks make a dramatic picture
—blue sky, grey rock, white glacier, green trees.

Hidden Cascades.
The roar of water fills my ears.
And wind in the trees.
It is beautiful and peaceful up here.
I cannot help but view this majesty and know
there must be some divine force.

I sit at the base of the falls,
cool drafts of air waft down from the water and refresh me.
I love waterfalls.
I can listen for hours to their mesmerizing cascades.
The water is snow-white from the falls.
Veils of mist spray out from the rocks.
I strain my neck upwards to catch it all in.

Yellowstone

I
Abyss Pool.
Small geysers all around,
bubbling mud, water pools.
Steam billows everywhere.
The aroma of sulfur and acid fills the air.
I feel the heat waft pass.

Heat and mineral turn the landscape a multi-colored portrait.
Sapphire-blue and green pools.
Bleached white soil.
Golds and yellows and browns and reds from mineral deposits.
Inanimate flower beds
reminding me of Teton wildflowers.
Purples, reds, blues, whites, yellows!
All so delicate!
All so beautiful!

II
I stand in front of Black Pool,
which is really a deep blue,
engulfed in warm sulfur steam.
Incredible!
The pool so deep, so clear.
I see strange underwater ridges that shimmer ghostly white
through crystal blue water.

The runoff flows towards Yellowstone Lake.
The edges of the pool are grey-white,
in sharp contrast to the blue water.
The runoff flows beneath me along that white course
yet to the sides, the ground is a bizarre pattern of browns
(browns that come in infinite shades from light to dark)
tans, golds, and yellows.

A ghostly, beautiful landscape, indeed.
The wind carries the steam past me;
I alternate sulfur hot and mountain cool.

Some holes are small and I cannot see water or mud
but I hear them percolate and bubble just out of sight.
Glug, glug, glug!
Bloop, bloop, bloop!

III
I enter the Central Plateau region.
It is early dawn and still cool.
The valley is grey mist and green grass.
The river unseen
save for shimmering arcs of sunlight
shining through the mist.
An incredible sight!
The mountains on all sides frame the scene in my mind.

I am at the top of the lower falls.
Can you hear the roar of the water?
It is deafening!
I feel the ground at my feet shake.
Do you?

An immense flow of water cascades over the falls.
As it begins its descent, the water shines a bright green
with the slightest hints of yellow.
But all color disappears into pure white below.

Water vapor billows up from the bottom.
The wind carries the mist up the canyon.

The canyon still volcanically active.
Steam vents shoot out all over the walls of the canyon.
The air hangs heavy with the scent of sulfur
(but where I am, the air is fresh and clean).

The early morning sun is still low.
The river and canyon snake east after the base of the falls.
The river shines in reflected light as it courses through the canyon
whose walls are yellow,
brown,
white,
black,
and gold with sulfur and iron deposits.
Pine trees protrude from the rock,
splashing their dark pine green into the picture.
It is all awesome!

SWOOP! SPLASH!
An osprey dives into the river just before the precipice.
It emerges with a gigantic fish in its talons.
The fish squiggles and squirms,
but to no avail.
As the osprey flies towards its canyon aerie,
the fish must contemplate its fate as the osprey's breakfast!

IV
I think I will sit in the shade.
When I first see Old Faithful erupt, I am but one of thousands,
all of us simultaneously snapping pictures and running video cameras.
And it is amazing to see.
A geyser erupting!
Water, super-heated by magma near the surface,
shooting hundreds of feet into the air.
Is there any more recognizable landmark of America's natural heritage?

Though some of the smaller geysers around Old Faithful
are more beautiful
with their multitude of colors.
Anemone Geyser:
two holes in the ground.

One suddenly fills up with water, starts bubbling,
and small jets of water shoot several feet into the air.
After a few minutes, it stops
and the water gurgles down the hole out of sight.
Several minutes later, its twin repeats the performance!

V
Sulfur cauldron.
A huge bubbling pool of pea-green sulfur water churning beneath me.
Billowy clouds of sulfur steam waft past me.
Nearby, a spot of ground sizzles from the heat just below the surface.
I am in awe!

VI
I drive from Yellowstone to Glacier—incredible!
Now I know why Montana is called the Big Sky country.
The land is vast!
Mountains on all horizons with low rolling land between.
I get vertigo from so much openness.

I detour past Headwaters of the Missouri State Park.
I wade out to the confluence of the three rivers that form the Missouri.
I do not care what others may say,
the Missouri seems much bigger than the Mississippi!

Glacier

I
I pause my solitary journey
and join seven strangers.
Six days of backcountry wilderness.

II
I sit in a meadow on the bank of the Belly River.
In front, mountain peaks jut up out of the trees.

Glaciers glisten white against the gray-black granite.
On either side, more mountain peaks!

Below the snow field, a waterfall cascades down
—a small gray line against the rock.
Directly in front, the river flows by.
The sound of water mixes with the wind in the trees.
Together they form a most tranquil sound.
A deer walks past us on the trail,
knowing it is safe here.

III
I am in a big field.
Mountains to our front and left.
In front is the Continental Divide.
Clouds pile up on the western side,
but it is nice and sunny here.

IV
Foot of Glenns Lake
The scenery is incredible!
Always through the trees, the mountains tower overhead.
Many still have snow packs on them.
It is the sides of the mountain that sustain life,
not the top.

V
Head of Glenns
Rain sets in.

Around the campfire, it is dry because of all the trees.
We sit around the fire, tell stories, and talk.

Our group:
Amy and Liz
—sisters or lovers or both

—an air about them straight out of a Bronte or Austen novel
—speaking a strange, forced accent
(I have heard it before, but I cannot place where).
Anne, from Brooklyn
—poet and yoga instructor
—hypoglycemic
—gets cold really quick
—has a great set of organically grown teas.
Tim, a software engineer from Austin
—two kids at home—four and six
—extroverted
—a big kid himself.
Steve is an accountant in Baltimore
—quiet.
Elena, my friend from law school
—fifteen years later, you will die from breast cancer
—we share a tent but lose touch after Glacier
—when I read the email saying you died, I am sad
—and I think of this time and how innocent it must seem.
Carolyn
—our guide
—Massachusetts by birth, Montanan by choice
—friendly and knowledgeable
—I wonder what you think of us?
—some groups are better, some are worse
—Of course, you will say we are one of the best
—what else would you say?

We are all different roads
and connect
and intersect
and affect each other in countless ways.
We are the sum of all those we meet
and with whom we interact.

Later, I sit in my sleeping bag listening to the rain on the tent walls,
the wind flapping and shaking the tent.
Everything I need to wear is damp.
I sit and think and question:
Why am I here?
Will I be famous?
Should I have left science for law?
Would I have thought up some new discovery?
$e^{i\pi} + 1 = 0$, what more proof does one need of God's existence?
$E = mc^2$.

Outside the camp, Glenns Lake twenty feet away.
It is cold and deep

The mountains tower all around us.
Across the lake, Cosley Mountain looms up into the sky.
Rocks and crags disappear into the mist.
Newly fallen snow peppers the rocks and cracks.
To the right, Stony Mountain Pass looms like a wall.
The snow pack ends in a waterfall.
Clouds hug the upper parts of the pass in their misty grasp.

The sisters are in the tent next to mine.
They laugh and giggle and talk in that strange accent.

VI
The sun comes out!
Sitting at the brink of a small waterfall fed out of Shepard Glacier.
The stream continuing on into narrow Glenns Lake,
which in turn feeds into Cosley Lake,
then the Belly River,
ultimately Hudson Bay.
White Crow Mountain to my left,
Cosley Mountain, on my right,
Mount Merritt and Pyramid Peak, on the far right.
Behind us the pass, above us the sun.

In front the Belly River valley.
Snow dusts the top of Merritt.
It is beautiful and awesome and incredible.

Rumble tumble the water
grumbles over the rock
down down down
over the rock
the water falls
splashing and dashing
washing the rock below.

VII
Stoney Indian Lake
I climb up the slope of Stoney Indian Peak above camp.
Stoney Indian Lake glimmers in emerald green.
The valley descends to my right
flanked on all sides by towering snow dusted peaks.
The sun filters through in a magical mid-afternoon glow.
I myself am in full sun
and shed my shirt to absorb the warmth
after two days of drenching rain.

The green water soothes me as I gaze down from my rock perch.
The water is clear and I can see every rock,
every stone that lies on the bottom.
The green mountain inspires me as I gaze up from my rock perch.
The air is clear and I can see every rock,
every stone that lies on top.

The lake is many shades of green.
The mountain is many shades of green,
but also grey and brown and yellow.
The air chills me now.
I move back towards the sun.

We see fossilized remains of some of the oldest life on earth
—a blue-green algae.
Ancestor to us all.

VIII
Kootenee Lakes
I plunge into freezing water,
chilled by glacial run off.
Now I lie on the warm grass,
warmed by the sun's golden rays.

Our thirty mile wilderness trek concludes at Waterton
where parting is such sweet sorrow.
We start as strangers,
but after six days in the Glacier back country,
we end as comrades.

Craters of the Moon

The moon rises over the Montana landscape.
Incredible!
Distant mountains ghostly in the dim moonlight
with broad rolling plains between.

I re-cross the border between Northwest and Southwest.
I am on an immense flat plateau.
To my right the Sawtooths tower overhead.
But to my left,
to the east,
that is spectacular.
Blue gray through the distant haze, snow-capped,
the Grand Tetons.
Even from a distance, their majesty and beauty
are something to behold.

Now I am on some other-worldly moon.
Everything black and crumbly and pumice and volcanic.
I hike into the very bowels of a crater.
The frozen river of lava is apparent.
I close my eyes and can almost hear the molten river
flow past so many years before.

And the sky.
Nary a cloud.
Bright, sunny, blue, dry.

Dinosaur National Monument

I
Lampore Canyon on the Green River

The Green River is brown today.
Flash floods muddy the water.
The canyon's red and black cliffs tower on both sides.
I camp on a little beach formed around a side canyon
created by a small creek.

I sit at the edge of the river.
The mud-brown water flows past.
The sound of water over rocks is a soothing music that fills me.
It is calm here at the water's edge.

II
Jones Hole Creek confluence with the Green River

Ute proverb: We are here not to destroy, but to be part of.
Travel gently and soak in the sounds of the ageless stream
and far-flung winds.
Walk in concert with those who will follow your footsteps
and with those whose footsteps you follow.

That is the true way,
the way towards inner peace and union and harmony with Nature.
Thereby uniting the divine with the mortal that resides within us all.

I see ancient petrographs.
Fascinating!
Paintings of animals and ghostly figures.
What do they mean?
What were those ancient peoples trying to say?
Why?
I try to understand.

I find a small waterfall.
I sit under its cool shower and refresh myself.
The cold water rushes over my body, hot from the day.

The trail runs along Jones Hole Creek,
a river I often imagine:
A small creek with cool, clear water gurgling and splashing over rocks.
On either side tall, cool shade trees,
and rocks perfect for sitting and thinking.
If only it ran through a broad rolling meadow of tall green grass
filled with bright multi-colored wildflowers,
with tall snow-capped peaks in the far distance
and soft tree covered mountains in the near distance.
Then it would be perfect.
I close my eyes and I see it.
I picture myself lying on the soft grass,
my feet dangling in the cool water.
Perhaps I have packed a small lunch
or perhaps I am accompanied by a friend
and we are discussing everything and nothing.

Ah, if only I could find that place,
my Garden of Eden.

Arches

I
Double Arch

Delicate and beautiful.
Will my poor words do justice to the majesty
and beauty of this landscape?
Brilliant red rock, arches, pillars, columns tower into the sky
stand in stark contrast to deep azure blue sky.
I look at the ruins of an ancient civilization.
I see the remnants of the once great city.
It is truly breathtaking.

Old Man: Close your eyes. What do you hear?
Young Man: I hear the water, I hear the birds.
Old Man: Do you hear your own heartbeat?
Young Man: No.
Old Man: Do you hear the grasshopper that is at your feet?
Young Man: No.
Young Man: Old Man, how is it that you hear these things?
Old Man: Young Man, how is it that you do not?

I am listening, Old Man.
And I hear these things.

II
Delicate Arch

Like pilgrims to Jerusalem,
we tread under the sweltering afternoon sky.
Our gaze never further than the next step.
For one and one half miles we walk
and we sweat
and we toil.
Always forward.

Always upward.
Until we round a rock wall and see it
—the Delicate Arch.

The Arch is on the edge of a large bowl-shaped rock formation.
As if by design, the opposite side of the bowl has a bench-like rim
on which we sit and rest our weary legs.

Why the trek?
Why our pilgrimage?
To see the fabled sunset at Delicate Arch.
More awesome than Mecca, it is.
We are told that God himself takes time out
to paint the colors on the rock and sky.
I hope it is so.

The sun begins its descent into night.
The crowd grows with anticipation.
Already the red rock seems a little more red.
The western horizon is yellow.
Shadows reach the base of the Arch.

The sun sets!
The red arch is now a dull brown.
The western horizon is ablaze.
The rocky fins and spires and columns
stand in stark silhouette
against the flame orange sky.
The clouds due west are yellow-orange.
While on either flank,
the color melds into bright lavender.

To the southwest, the silhouette of Balanced Rock
glows a dull red.
The clouds due south are orange.

The rays of the now-gone sun can barely be seen as shafts of light emanating from below the horizon.

The sky darkens.
The crowd departs for the slow descent,
renewed and refreshed.
And "with wand'ring steps and slow,
through Eden took their solitary way."

III
I awake to the sunrise.
Spectacular!
Just outside my tent.

Grand Canyon

Sitting in a rocking chair on the patio of the Grand Canyon Lodge,
I watch a storm over the south rim.
The rain in silver-grey veils descends from the clouds.
Low rumbles of thunder drift past.
Yellow forks of lightning flash through the rain veils.

Off in the southern distance a wildfire blazes.
Lightning started it several days ago.
Perhaps the rain will put it out.

Zion

I
Angels Point

I am on the edge of the world
2000 feet above the valley floor.
I climb up and around the cliff face

relying on chains and chiseled foot holds.
Incredible!

All the world is below
only sky and rock above.

It is a truly humbling experience to be up here.
When the hubris of mankind looms too large,
I will think of this place.
How tiny we are.
How miniscule and insignificant when compared to
the awesome size
and majesty
and beauty
of these rocks
and canyons
and stones
and river
and sky
and cloud
and earth
and cosmos.
I gaze out from my aerie perch
and am filled with an overwhelming sense of wonder.

Truly a divine spirit resides out here.
These cliff towers are its temple.
But it also resides within.
Ascend the narrow canyons of the soul,
and gaze out at the wonder and mystery of the divine inside.
To understand our role in the scheme of nature and wonder,
to know our place and our function,
to be one with nature not against nature,
to be a part of nature not apart from nature
—could that be the secret to true happiness?

II
I hike to Observation Point.
A mile to go, it rains.
A half mile to go, it pours.
A quarter mile to go, a tempest!
I round a corner and I am hit by a wall of water and wind
—a white wall of wet.
Lightning and thunder crash all around me.
I turn around and hurry back to the north face.
I take shelter under a rock overhang.
It is incredible!
Clinging to the rock in the middle of raging tempest.

The lightning passes and the rain lightens.
I start down.
My descent is halted in a narrow canyon where a flashflood
makes continuing impossible.
Fellow hikers sit waiting for the water level to lower.
The canyon floor was dry when I started,
now it is a raging flood.
An hour passes in pleasant conversation until the water recedes
enough to trudge in knee-deep water and continue down.

III
I hike a bit up the Narrows,
a canyon of the Virgin River.
The trail is the river.
I walk up the river, splashing about.
The water is fast and deep because of yesterday's storm.
More are forecast for today,
so I only walk a few miles and turn back.

The cliffs and canyons,
the water and rock are too awesome!
Zion is an incredible place.

Olympics

I
Rialto Beach

I sit on a large piece of driftwood
waiting for the sun to set on the Pacific Ocean.
The place is alive and wild.
Rock islands jut out from the rocky beach.
Tidal pools filled with anemone and starfish.
The former are delicate pale green,
the latter a rainbow of orange and red and black and brown.

It is good that I have come here at the end of my journey.
The Pacific fills me with a sense of fruition.
I have satisfied my own manifest destiny.
I have been East and North and South and West.
Now the Pacific.
I am at the edge of the continent,
I am at the end of the world as I know it, and I feel fine.

Staring at the setting sun,
I reflect on my spirit of manifest destiny,
my desire, my need to go to the end of all there is
and to explore that limit.
My body is awash in the red light of dusk,
and my feet are awash in the cold Pacific waters.
Left solely to my thoughts.
I have seen beautiful mountains,
majestic canyons,
and awe-inspiring vistas.
And there is no end to the exploration.
There is always something just over the horizon.
And there is always something new in the places already visited,
even if it is merely a subtle new way
to look at something once thought familiar

but now cast in a totally foreign light.
How exhilarating it is!
How human it feels!
How divine it enables us to become!

II
Hurricane Ridge (Mountain Solitaire)

Hiking alone
is a soul refreshing experience.
Although hiking with companions is also nice in its own way,
there is nothing quite like solo hiking.

When hiking I become part of the nature about me.
On a mountain, the land of earth and the land of sky
meet at the mountaintop.
Hiking that ridge places me on the hazy borderland
between the two realms of earth and sky.
Sometimes the trail descends down into the valleys and hollows
and I am surrounded by the mountain realm.
Other times, the trail juts out onto cliffs
and for a brief moment I enter the realm of sky.
All around is sky
and cloud
and blue,
save for the small sliver of rock at my feet,
which reminds me of my roots to the realm of earth.

But for those brief moments,
I am on top of the world,
immersed in the clouds
and wind
and nothingness
of the heavens.

I like hiking alone.
There is no unnatural sound.
No other voices to distract my mind from my surroundings.
I stop.
All there is is the sound of the wind through the trees,
the creak of the fir trunks,
the buzz of the insects,
the chirp of the bird.
Sometimes even these become non-existent
and all is quiet,
all is still.

I start walking.
I add to this melody of sound new sounds.
The sound of my breathing.
The soft swoosh-swish of my water bottle.
But mostly it is the dull
thump thump thump
of my boots on the trail,
a metronymic cadence
that hypnotizes me as I walk.

I pass another solitary hiker.
Our eyes meet.
We nod.
We tip our hats.
We pass one another as we continue on our meditative treks.
No words are spoken but we have spoken volumes.
How hard was he breathing?
Was he sweaty?
What condition were his boots and clothes?
What was he carrying?
These things say all that is necessary,
without the need to shatter the silence of the hike
or the quiet contemplation of the hikers.

III
Hoh Rainforest

Beautiful are the rainforests of the Olympic Peninsula!
The greenest greens and the brownest browns.
Huge trees and long flowing moss.
It is everything I think a rainforest should be
and nothing like what I expect.

Olympic Hot Springs.
Seven primitive hot tubs.
No more than a pile of rocks damming a hot spring
forming pools.
The first is the hottest.
The seventh, the largest.

I become primitive and soak au naturel.
I hike up,
strip down,
leave all pride crumpled up with my clothes on a rock,
step into the hot mineral water,
and sit down in the mud on a submerged rock.

There are six of us—three men and three women
(though I know no one).
Our nakedness is not an issue.
People stand up and move to another part of the pool
while the conversation continues as if we are in a café
having coffee and tea.
Eyes never glance away in embarrassment.
Why should they?
We are created unclothed,
we should not be ashamed of our humanity.

Mount Rainier

14,000 feet of rock and snow and ice and glacier.
My trail is rock and snow and wildflowers!
A rainbow of Indian paintbrush and lungwort.

A host of vibrant, multi-colored flowers growing out of the alpine tundra.
At lunch, I watch climbers ascend the summit.

I pass several streams.
Milky white from the rock flour
—it is beautiful!
The glacier is amazing.
Snow and ice packed so thick,
the water crystals realign into sheets so that the mass can move.
A white river,
a river of ice.
At its base, a mass of rock and earth, plowed by the snow.
Rivulets of melting snow flow from the base.

The august glacier is a mass of broken ice.
Crevasses glow in an eerie ice-blue light.
Radiating it seems, although it is really just the reflection of sun and sky.
At least that is what the rangers say.

The next day, the sky is cloudy.
Rainier rises like an island above the cloud
—incredible!

Somewhere over eastern Colorado or western Kansas

The flight home.
The sun is setting
or the earth is spinning,

depending upon your particular point of view.
We pass through a cloud,
surrounded by a dull red and pink haze
as the cloud is back-lit by the setting sun.

The horizon a flat horizontal rainbow:
red at the horizon followed by
orange
yellow
green
blue
then the violet of night.
Below, aluminum grey clouds
form a blanket over the darkened earth.
In my imagination,
I scamper along that fluffy-soft pseudo-surface below.
In my imagination.

Coda

Mountain, desert, forest, ocean,
I am ready to go home.

Certain memories stand out,
and I feel guilty.
I do not wish to disparage the others by singling out a few.
Every moment is spectacular,
and exciting,
and new.

I inhale great draughts of space,
The east and the west are mine,
and the north and the south are mine.

I am larger, better than I thought,
I did not know I held so much goodness.

All seems beautiful to me.

Appalachian Dawn

Black mountains loom all around me.
Trees fade into the mist
in the dark purple sky of the growing dawn.
I think that when God is not in heaven,
He is here
in the cool pre-dawn hours
in the heart of the Appalachians.

The growing light turns the trees a grayish green.
Mountains loom in front and fade into the gray fog of low-lying clouds.
The road is a light gray ribbon,
slicing through the scene.
The music playing on my radio permeates the scene,
the Chameleons, I think.

I come across a small mountain farm.
A brick fireplace and chimney rise from the tall grass
like a pillar.
Alone.
A marker for a life and a world that once was.
Who were they?
When did they live?
Did they have the same wants and desires and joys and fears?
Did they feel love and pain, know religion and peace?

I cross Monterey Mountain.
I am engulfed by fog.
Morning has definitely arrived
though the sky is overcast.
I see a tall solitary tree through the fog, hauntingly beautiful.
No colors,
only a grey-black silhouette in a silvery cloud.

I travel on
and stop beside a small, unnamed river near Cheat Mountain.
It occurs to me that this river will slowly flow to the Kanawha River

which flows into the Ohio.
The Ohio, of course, feeds into the Mississippi at Cairo
and then South to New Orleans
and the Gulf of Mexico.
I look at water that will eventually flow past
a bench in New Orleans.
A bench where I once sat and spent a wonderful time
with a beautiful woman.
A beautiful woman I once loved.
I wonder what couple will be sitting on that bench
when the water I am watching flows by.

I continue my journey through daybreak.
I think I see God.
Valley in the foreground, mountains in the back.
Fog in the mountains.
Blue sky above.
Clouds.
The sun bursts through the cloud
sending shafts of light to the ground.
I see it:
the central white light,
the orb of the sun
radiating its brilliance, its light, its life, to the earth below.
It is magical.
I stop and frantically write.
Try to express my thoughts into words,
my words into squiggles and marks on paper.
Constantly I gaze at the scene.
Is it real?
Truly this is religion
and it cannot be found in any four walls.

Finally Gaudineer Knob, my destination.
The scene is eerie but mystically romantic.
Surrounded by trees and fog.

The nearer trees are green
as trees should be in summer.
But green melds into grey into black into white fog
as the trees advance up the mountain.

The forest floor is a random pattern,
black dirt, grey boulders, brown pine needles and green moss.
Trees so thick I can scarcely look along any line of sight
without a tree being in my view.
Is this what the pioneers saw?
Am I looking at the same view early settlers or first peoples saw?
I am surrounded by a silvery veil of mist.
I have found my religion.
A religion that cannot be defined,
that cannot be confined.
A religion whose God is found in the Appalachian dawn.
A religion whose God is heard in the soft hiss of snow
falling on a quiet river
on a snowy night.
A religion that accepts us for who we are:
good people, trying to do good,
even when we stumble and fall.

One of the greatest sins, I think, is not taking the time,
even if for but a moment,
to enjoy the beauty of one's surroundings.
Whether those surroundings are the Appalachians at dawn,
or the ocean's shore at dusk,
or a city skyline at night,
or a beautiful woman.

I try to think of these things often,
so as to not be considered guilty of such a sin.

Hailing from the Tidewater region of Virginia, **Gregory Ashe** grew up along the banks of the mighty Lynnhaven River. When not spending time on the river or at the beach, Greg spent many a summer camping at Big Meadows in Shenandoah National Park, Seashore State Park in Virginia Beach, and Lake Gaston in North Carolina. Now, he is a father of three, husband to one, government consumer protection lawyer, former astronomy student, and observer of life.

A Renaissance man, Greg obtained his undergraduate degree in astronomy and physics with a minor in history and a graduate degree in astronomy before setting his sights on the law. While in academia, Greg authored or co-authored several scientific and legal articles, including "Steady State Cooling Flow Models with Gas Loss for Normal Elliptical Galaxies," 345 *The Astrophysical Journal*, 22-30 (1989); "Modeling the Structure of H I in the Galactic Disk," 409 *The Astrophysical Journal*, 682 (1993); and "Reflecting the Best of Our Aspirations: Protecting Modern and Post-Modern Architecture," 15 *Cardozo Arts & Entertainment Law Journal* 69 (1997). Meanwhile, his poetry has appeared in *Fredericksburg Literary and Art Review* and *Penultimate Peanut*.

When not protecting consumers, Greg enjoys camping, reading, listening to music, and competing in marathons and ultramarathons. He lives with his family in the Washington, D.C. suburbs.

This is Greg's first published book of poetry.

www.ingramcontent.com/pod-product-compliance
Lightning Source LLC
LaVergne TN
LVHW041553070426
835507LV00011B/1074